# NONRELIGIOUS
# CHRISTIANITY

Also available in the Pioneer *Perspectives* series:

| | |
|---|---|
| Better Than or Equal To? | Linda Harding |
| Caring for New Christians | Margaret Ellis |
| Christian Citizenship | Mike Morris |
| Crossing Cultures | Paul Dakin |
| Healing Then and Now | Martin Scott |
| Out of the Ghetto and Into the City | Patrick Dixon |
| The Power to Persuade? | Cleland Thom |
| Prophecy in the Church | Martin Scott |
| Radical Evangelism | Pete Gilbert |
| Relationships—Jesus Style | Stuart Lindsell |
| The Role and Ministry of Women | Martin Scott |
| The Worshipping Church | Noel Richards |
| Your Mind Matters | Chris Seaton |

For further information on the Pioneer *Perspectives* series and Pioneer, please write to:

P.O. Box 79c, Esher, Surrey, KT10 9LP

# NONRELIGIOUS CHRISTIANITY

## Gerald Coates

**WORD PUBLISHING**
Nelson Word Ltd
Milton Keynes, England

WORD AUSTRALIA
Kilsyth, Australia

NELSON WORD CANADA
Vancouver, B.C., Canada

STRUIK CHRISTIAN BOOKS (PTY) LTD
Cape Town, South Africa

JOINT DISTRIBUTORS SINGAPORE—
ALBY COMMERCIAL ENTERPRISES PTE LTD
and
CAMPUS CRUSADE, ASIA LTD

PHILIPPINE CAMPUS CRUSADE FOR CHRIST
Quezon City, Philippines

CHRISTIAN MARKETING NEW ZEALAND LTD
Havelock North, New Zealand

JENSCO LTD
Hong Kong

SALVATION BOOK CENTRE
Malaysia

NONRELIGIOUS CHRISTIANITY

Copyright © Pioneer 1995.

Published by Nelson Word Ltd./Pioneer 1995.

All rights reserved.

ISBN 0-85009-738-X

Unless otherwise indicated, Scripture quotations are from the HOLY BIBLE, NEW INTERNATIONAL VERSION, copyright © 1973, 1978, 1984 by International Bible Society.

Front cover illustration: *Afternoon Tea*, Susan Kuznitsky, by courtesy of Felix Rosenstiel's Widow and Son Ltd., London.

Reproduced, printed and bound in Great Britain for Nelson Word Ltd. by Cox and Wyman Ltd., Reading.

95 96 97 98 / 10 9 8 7 6 5 4 3 2 1

# FOREWORD

Pioneer *Perspectives* are perhaps more than their title suggests!

They are carefully researched presentations of material, on important issues, appealing to thinking churches, creative leaders and responsible Christians.

Each *Perspective* pioneers in as much as it is at the cutting edge of biblical and theological issues. Each will continue to pioneer with new ideas, concepts and data drawn from Scripture, history and a contemporary understanding of both.

They are perspectives in as much as they aim to be an important contribution to the ongoing debate on issues such as women in ministry and leadership; prophets and prophecy in the church; biblical models of evangelism; integrating and discipling new believers; growing and building local churches and further perspectives on Christ's second coming.

Importantly, these studies use a journal style of presentation, and are written by people who are currently working out the implications of the issues they are writing about, in local churches. This is vital if we are to escape the dangerous fantasy of abstract theology without practical experience. They are not written to contribute to the paralysis of analysis—rather to feed, strengthen, nurture and inform so that we can be equipped to get God's will done, by networking the nations with the gospel using all the resources that are available to us.

God's Word is always an event. How much we thank

Him that He has left us an orderly account of what He wants us to believe, how He wants us to live, and what He wants us to do in order to bring heaven to the earth. As we embrace a better understanding of Scripture, rooted in local church, national and international mission, we shall become a part of the great eschatological purpose of bringing back the King—not for a church defeated, cowering and retiring but for one which, despite colossal odds, pressures and persecutions, is faithful to her Lord and His Word.  To do that we must 'search the Scriptures' to see if many of these 'new things' are true.  I commend these *Perspectives* to you as they are published on a regular basis throughout these coming years.

Gerald Coates
Director Pioneer Trust/Team Leader

**Pioneer** consists of a team of men and women and network of churches, committed to dynamic and effective biblical Christianity.

The national team act as advisers and consultants to churches, which in many cases develop into a Partnership with the Pioneer team. These are the churches keen to identify with the theology, philosophy, ethos and purpose of Pioneer. The team have a vigorous youth ministry, church-planting strategy and evangelistic emphasis.

Training courses include the highly successful Equipped to Lead and TIE teams (Training In Evangelism).

Pioneer has also been instrumental in initiating and funding March for Jesus (with Ichthus/YWAM); the AIDS initiative which became known as ACET (AIDS Care Education Training); and Pioneer Romania Aid.

Pioneer works in many countries around the world in evangelism, church planting and leaders' conferences.

# ACKNOWLEDGEMENTS

Each Pioneer *Perspective* draws from a wide range of sources and commentators and Scripture itself.

This Perspective is no different.

I wish to record my gratitude to the following people for thoughts and ideas which have helped shape this publication: Ravi Zacharias, Malcolm Muggeridge, Stuart Lindsell, Chris Bourne, William De Arteaga, Dr Patrick Dixon, Martin Scott, Roger Forster, Ern Baxter, John Noble and Eugene H. Peterson.

And to all those rare souls whom I have met—non-religious lovers of Christ our Saviour.

Gerald Coates
Esher, Surrey
Spring 1995

# CONTENTS

# CHAPTER 1

# A CONTRADICTION IN TERMS?

## Part One: Setting the Scene

Nonreligious Christianity? Surely the very phrase is a contradiction in terms?

Isn't Christianity another religion, albeit a superior religion? Certainly that is what the majority of people believe throughout Western Europe, the Americas and beyond. But in the 'beyond' some would not even regard it as superior, never mind unique.

Part of this is because Europe, of which my nation is a part, has lost her way and her identity. Priding ourselves on 'religious tolerance' we have no spiritual convictions. Tolerance is a panacea to all our ills until eventually we tolerate the intolerable. For example, if you were to write a letter to a friend asking them to ensure the murder of someone who offended you, the police would be more than interested. But in the name of expediency, and no doubt a small amount of fear, police can be fully aware that Muslim leaders have endorsed the death sentence of someone who has offended them, costing the nation millions of pounds in protection. It seems nothing is done about it.

The monarchy and the Government and major sections of the church parade around in a swamp of confusion regarding belief and practice. In so doing they fail to give a lead as to core values for the nation.

Meanwhile the Muslim communities all over the world are finding their identity and extreme sections are expressing it with bombs and bullets.

The majority of Muslims in the UK work hard, pay taxes and get on with their faith and relationships in the privacy of their homes and mosques. Nevertheless, the Muslim community is finding an identity with mosques being built across the UK in prime positions in city after city, with many women now wearing head coverings and a number of media personalities using their new Muslim names. A classic example is Cat Stephens.

And apart from silence, fear, and sometimes even the notion that all of this is really not important, what is the Christian response?

Apart from religious tolerance, occasionally peppered with an appropriate but nevertheless predictable condemnation of extremists seeing so much blood shed—nothing! Why? Because as Christians we are either embarrassed by our identity and history or, as is often the case, completely lacking in a knowledge of historical identity. Evangelical individualism with its personal emphasis on quiet times, holiness, Bible reading and witness rob us of any sense of corporate identity, purpose and mission. This ground must be regained if we are to be anything other than 'socially irrelevant if privately engaging'.[1] Whilst the Muslim communities in the UK quietly practise their faith primarily in cities, Islam has a vice-like grip in many nations of the world. News of beatings, torture, crucifixion and other forms of execution are continually filtering out through secret letters, reports and occasional visitors. The Jubilee Campaign has for a long time been representing our brothers and sisters in these nations.

---

1   Theodore Ruszak, *Where the Wasteland Ends* (Doubleday).

## Religion and the West

But this is not the only threat to the church. Interactive computers will give all children and teenagers, as well as adults, access to a range of entertainment undreamed of, not to mention pornography. Sport is set to create a commitment of time and finance that many churches only dream of. The medical world no longer regards itself as upholding Christian morality and the sanctity of life. Abortion on demand is virtually the norm and euthanasia has gone on in many parts of Europe for years. Educationalists have 'educated us into imbecility', as Malcolm Muggeridge put it, where children barely know the difference between right and wrong. Court cases could lead one to believe that the burglar has as many rights as the burgled, the murderer as the murdered.

But what has all this got to do with religion or non-religious Christianity? Everything.

In my lifetime most Western nations have been secularised, pluralised and privatised. The Oxford Dictionary defines these words as follows:

*SECULAR* adj. Concerned with the affairs of this world, worldly; not sacred; not monastic or ecclesiastical; temporal, profane, lay; sceptical of religious truth or opposed to religious education.
*PLURAL* adj. Denoting more than one.
*PLURALISM* n. System that recognises more than one principle.
*PRIVATE* adj. Kept removed from public knowledge; not open to the public; one's own; individual, personal, not affecting the community; confidential.

So there we have it, entire people groups within the nations of the Western world who have been secularised, pluralised and privatised. In the areas of the media, art, medicine and education, let alone Government and monarchy, there is no room for a vibrant *faith*, but simply the trappings of *religion*. God, His word and His ways are not acknowledged, never mind obeyed. Christianity is seen as one of many religions. The media, whilst refraining from any criticism of the Muslim community and even the Hindu community, blaspheme and ridicule Christ and Christians every night on TV. And the general notion within the community is that Christianity is to be kept private—it shouldn't affect issues like abortion, euthanasia, homosexuality, but is allowed to affect the poor and suffering. Of course opponents will be quick to add, and rightly so, that one does not have to be a Christian to care for the poor and the suffering.

Religion in my lifetime seems to have been defenceless against this onslaught. How will it fare in the future? I think badly. And this is not to criticise the many hardworking, faithful, sincere and born-again people within 'Christian' religious systems.

But it is my contention that the Christian religion has made Christ unattractive and unintelligible. How has this happened? We shall have to go back to find a brighter future.

## Part Two: Religion and Ancient Writings

There certainly seems to be a complete lack—indeed, not even a hint—of religion in the opening chapters of Genesis. Fun and friendship, sexual compatibility, an open heaven and open relationships mark what little we know of those times.

But after sin, wrongdoing and violence entered into the world of time and space, it seems the growing population became more and more religious.

Society became divided into different languages, creeds, religions and systems of beliefs and morality. It looked as though God had abandoned the cosmos and all the people groups in it. After Adam failed, things got so bad that God decided to destroy His creation. God started again through Noah's family. But it all went wrong again. What was God to do?

## A promise of commitment

Abraham was a descendant of Shem and the son of Terah who became the ancestor of the Hebrew (Jewish) nations (Genesis 17:5). He lived a life of remarkable faith and was known as the 'friend of God' (2 Chronicles 20:7). The biblical narrative continues through his son Isaac and then Isaac's son Jacob.

Abraham and his descendants became God's chosen minority to bless the majority, all the nations of the earth. God never blesses the minority to curse the majority but uses that minority whether it be one, like Abraham, or many, like the Jewish people, to bless the majority. This happened eventually on the day of Pentecost when thousands of the descendants of Abraham were converted and baptised in the Holy Spirit. This was to swiftly bless all nations, both Jews and non-Jews, the Gentiles.

Jew was a term which originally described an inhabitant of Judah. It was primarily used by non-Jews to refer to the Hebrews, the descendants of Abraham. The New Testament would use the word Jew as a familiar term for all Israelites, those living in Israel.

The Old Testament therefore is the history of God's commitment to a people, to so fill them up with His love, life, law and awe-inspiring miracles that God would break out of that community and bless the nations of the earth. God gave His chosen people many things they requested, although it is questionable whether these were His original intentions. Later in her history Israel wanted a King. Among their reasons was that other people groups had kings and figureheads. Later still David wanted to build a temple for God. Other religions had temples, so why not the Jewish religion?  But it is highly questionable whether this was what God intended.

Back to Abraham!  God certainly gave faith to Abraham, as well as hope and provision. The same could be said of his son Isaac, whose name means laughter. And even the twister Jacob, Isaac's son, gets in on the act, revealing that God's grace and mercy and His willingness to forgive seem unending.

But prior to the time of Moses there was virtually nothing written down regarding how God wanted His followers to live. Sin had corrupted God's creation. But extraordinary people of faith, and even occasional failure, were able to hear from God, receive from God and model grace and truth to those around them. This early period of Israel's history should not be idealised.

## A new beginning?

Eventually the great Captivity took place and after many decades Moses led them out and in a sense a new history was about to begin. Written laws were then given. We know them as the Ten Commandments.

The first five books of the Bible, traditionally attributed to Moses, became the Pentateuch. This of course included the Ten Commandments. As a result of these books and the written law the priests gave directives relating to a wide range of behaviour within the religious community. Study of the Pentateuch and the law within it led to the 'oral tradition'. Alongside these sacred writings, including the law, emerged the interpretation of the law. It has been calculated that there were about 613 actual commandments—248 positive and 365 negative. These were then protected by the making of new laws which became known as 'making a hedge about the Torah'.[2]

The followers of Jehovah became networked in a labyrinth of law and legislation, written and oral traditions. The latter became as important as the former.

The influence of the Torah (the whole body of law and sacred writings) on the community was considerable. The books of Judges, Samuel and Kings recorded history from the viewpoint of the Torah, including times of obedience as well as times of neglect of the Torah. They saw the former as bringing blessing and the latter calamity.

Psalm 1 when speaking of the law is referring to the whole of the law, written and oral. Divine law is often acknowledged and indeed praised as the gauge by which a person's godliness is measured (Proverbs 28:4–7).

When God's people saw the Torah, God's law, as divine instruction from a merciful God who cares for His people, things seemed to go well relationally, medically and in many other respects. But once that heart condition was lost, the God who lives and speaks out of mercy and kindness disappeared behind legal sentences, commentaries and interpretation. Life-giving faith gave way to just another religion.

Of course amidst all of this growing legislation, which often became legalism, there was the issue of temple worship and ceremony.

2 *New Bible Dictionary* (IVP, 1962), page 672.

Some of the earliest structures built by human beings were temples or shrines where they could worship their God. The Tower of Babel is the first structure recorded in Scripture which implied the existence of a temple (Genesis 11:4). Although the Tower was intended to be a place where human beings could find God, it certainly symbolised the arrogant confidence of humanity attempting to reach heaven.

After Israel had grown into a nation, a central shrine became more than a desire. It was to be a gathering point for the people, a symbol of their unity. During the wilderness struggle they had a tabernacle. But now they wanted something more than that. Perhaps King David felt guilty when he acknowledged, 'Here I am, living in a palace of cedar, while the ark of God remains in a tent.' Nathan the prophet replied, 'Whatever you have in mind, go ahead and do it, for the Lord is with you.' That night God spoke to Nathan regarding His prophetic purposes, which were far greater than David building a house for Him. Perhaps David could not have been expected to fully understand the prophetic revelation (2 Samuel 7).

It is largely acknowledged that because David was stained with the blood of his enemies he was only allowed to collect materials and treasures and purchase the site. But he saw nothing but the foundation go down. It was to be his son Solomon who saw the actual construction of the temple, which was completed in seven years (1 Kings 6:37–38). It stood on the east side of the old city of Jerusalem, though its precise location is less certain. Nothing of Solomon's structure remains above the ground today, though it is likely that the work of levelling the rock and building up the great walls for the courtyard of Herod's temple obliterated earlier constructions. However, in 587 BC, three centuries after its construction, the temple was looted by Nebuchadnezzar, and was by all accounts in a considerable state of disrepair even prior to this disaster.

Ezekiel gave God's people plans for a temple although this was never built. Then a second temple was erected which stood for almost 500 years, longer than either the first or Herod's temple which was to follow. These two temples were places of sacrifice, worship and prayers, the making of promises as well as the confession of sin.

Herod's temple was started in 19 BC. It was simply an attempt to reconcile Jews to the monarchy, rather than to glorify God. The main structure was finished within ten years. Work continued on it until AD 64! This incredible structure, made of cream stone and gold, was barely finished before it was destroyed by the Romans in AD 70.

## Jewish religion and the future

In the next chapter we shall look at how both Jesus and the early apostles worshipped at the temple of Jerusalem. But the apostles hinted that the new order that Christ came to bring would disempower temple religion—in the priestly way of doing things, Stephen's defence of the faith could certainly have been interpreted as an attack on the temple.

The other issue which the Lord Jesus Christ faced over and over again was the issue of law. From Christ's teaching, Paul's revelation that we were either 'under law' or 'under grace' was to shatter people's religion as it was then understood. We know that God was the law-giver who in Christ became the law-keeper on the earth, who now by the outpoured Spirit keeps the law of love towards God and our neighbours in our heart. But this was a shattering revelation to those early church leaders and in fact was to become the biggest first-century church issue.

How could one honour the law, written and oral, and the temple way of doing things and apparently do away with it at the same time? It seemed to be the abolition of everything that God-fearing, God-honouring Judaism held dear.

By now of course a network of synagogues had been built. The word came to refer to the building in which worshippers gathered, although in its original meaning it simply denotes a gathering of people without any specific purpose. Historians argue that the importance of the synagogue to Judaism cannot be overestimated. It gave character to the Jewish faith and brought people in touch with their religious leaders. But there was no altar within the synagogue and eventually prayer and the reading of the Torah took the place of sacrifice. It was also a place where people gathered to discuss important affairs. In fact Dr Luke indicates in his record of the early church the significant role the synagogues played in networking the Jewish community with the gospel.

But neither the Old nor New Testament gives us any definitive information as to the origins of the synagogue.


## Conclusion

There is no way we can do justice to 39 books of the Old Testament in less then 39 pages. But Abraham, Isaac, Jacob and Moses were key figures in the early history of God's people. The writing down of the first five books of the Bible, the giving of the law and then the putting together of the interpretation of those laws became known as the Torah and Talmud. This, to a greater or lesser degree, guided the Israelites in what we know as the Old Testament. There were times of revival matched at times by unspeakable ungodliness. Holiness and harmony were decades later matched by pride and promiscuity. Throughout it all God extends grace through prophets and priests, kings and heroes. But prophets continually hinted at something better than sacrifice for sin, temple worship and living under the law.

Just as only a few ever embraced the idea of a suffering Messiah, or a saviour who would hang upon a tree (they had a theology for those who hung upon trees!) few if any understood the radical implications of Christ's coming with regard to law, temple worship and, by implication, religion.

But it should not be forgotten that when the people of God were living according to His law and were honouring God in temple worship, others took notice. When the unnamed Queen of Sheba went to Jerusalem to test Solomon's wisdom, a journey of some 1,200 miles, she was 'overwhelmed'. She was impressed not only with his wisdom, the food on his table, his colossal wealth but the fact that he worshipped the Lord. Equally astounding to her was the 'seating of his officials' when no doubt in her domain they stood! The whole place spoke not only of material wealth but of relational harmony and prosperity. Just imagine the stories that she and her courtiers would take home with them.

The Old Testament is the story of God looking for a person in Adam, Noah's family and Abraham's generations (with which the Old Testament is primarily concerned). God's desire was that through the law, and the grace He offered through ceremony and sacrifice, they should find their right place with Him and one another. The prophetic utterances, peppered throughout major parts of the Old Testament, lead us to believe that God's law, God's ways, God's glory, His grace, mercy and truth will eventually break out into the nations of the earth. The sum total of law and laws, ceremony and form which we may call the Jewish religion at times gave them happiness and holiness, revival and revelation. But without allowing for these means of grace, to touch one's heart, they merely became religious burdens and laws which caused people to judge each other when not adhered to, and then to isolate each other. Into this scene of hard hearts and religious taboos where the Talmud— the interpretation of the law—was put on the same level as the Ten Commandments, Jesus came.

And what a coming!

# CHAPTER 2

# JESUS AND RELIGION

We have seen in the previous chapter that God is primarily interested in people and relationships. The writers of the Old Testament scriptures are keen for us to see Israel's failures as well as her high and holy days. Relationships are key to both.

But as the world around them became more complex and the temptations more blatant, law and ceremony provided instruction and guidelines for maintaining relationships with God and one another.

Scripture clearly teaches that not all tradition is good, as we shall see in this chapter, though Paul himself did pass on traditions which he expected to be upheld.

But into a very traditional, conservative and religious scene was born a baby who was eventually to blow tradition, ceremony and what was perceived as Jewish religion sky high.

Many attempts have been made to disprove the birth and life of Christ. But not only is the whole New Testament based upon the life, death and resurrection of Christ, but the entire mission of the Christian church and, one could argue, world history has been affected by that one solitary life.

Earlier this century so-called 'high scholasticism' attempted to debunk the Scriptures historically, geographically and in terms of their accuracy particularly with regard to Christ. But Christianity came to be unique because of Christ. Christ claimed to be the son of God who could not only forgive and cleanse but impart a new Spirit, a new heart for a new beginning and ultimately a new world. Attack Christ and you are attacking the very heart of Christianity. Christianity is not, as we shall see, merely a set of rational propositions and moral ideals.

Evangelicalism was rocked in the 1940s by these attacks. But this higher scholasticism, originating in Germany with its modernity and latterly liberalism has emptied churches throughout Europe and indeed the Western world. Many of those liberals including Don Cupitt are now atheists. Some even like to call themselves 'atheistic Christians'. To me that is rather like saying that you are a 'beefburger-eating vegetarian'. I suppose if you are a senior leader in the church you are a 'cattle-owning vegetarian'!

Despite the fact that evangelicals have recently been the only growing wing of the church in the United Kingdom and indeed Europe and the Americas, there has always been an underlying scepticism about the accuracy of scripture. On Christmas Eve 1994 *The Times* newspaper gave a front-page story to Dr Carsten Thiede, the German papyrologist. In a scholarly journal he made a series of astonishing claims for fragments of *Magdalene Gr 17* which in the words of the journalist 'may transform our understanding of Christianity and the gospel'. Colleagues of mine told me that any theologian worth his or her salt had understood what Dr Carsten Thiede discovered years ago. Nevertheless it was an interesting development for the sceptics. His findings were simple. He argued that the Magdalene papyrus, a few verses of Matthew thought to date from the late second century, are not a second-century version but an eye-witness account! In other words it was written and read by men who walked with Christ through Galilee and wept as the storm gathered about Golgotha.

The early church claimed that the gospels were indeed written by Christ's disciples or by their followers. But the scholarship of the early twentieth century endeavoured to demolish these claims. There still lurks in many Christian minds the big question: 'What if the Bible is not true?' Doubt, as someone has said, need not be the enemy of the Christian, but can enable us to come to a knowledge of the truth. If we could not doubt we could never know the truth. We would have to accept it at face value.[1]

It should not be forgotten that Christianity was one of many religious groups originating in the Roman world. As it is today, so it was then—little interest was taken in this story until conflict arose. When that conflict emerged, writers such as Tacitus, Suetonius and Pliny all mention that Christ was the founder of Christianity.

## Historical accuracy

The late J. M. Geldenhuys BA, BD, Th.M. has noted that there are a number of indirect references to Christ in rabbinical writing which 'make reasonably recognisable mention of Him' as a transgressor in Israel who practised magic, scorned the words of the wise and led the people astray.[2] He noted that some had said He had come to add to the law, heal the sick in His name and was hanged on Passover eve.

Interestingly not even the bitterest enemies of Christianity had any notion of denying that Jesus had been born, lived and died in Palestine, or that He performed signs and wonders. Indeed both His death

1   1 Kings 10:1–10;  2 Chronicles 9:1–9
2   *New Bible Dictionary* (IVP, 1962), page 620.

and resurrection 'must be reckoned among the best established facts of history' according to Geldenhuys.

It is also important to note that the Acts of the Apostles, the Epistles and Revelation are all built on the fact that Jesus was born, lived, died and rose again.

The staggering thing is that the writers of the four gospels recorded not only many of these facts (though their prime purpose was to proclaim the good news rather than write factual biographies), but also, and in some detail, the continual run-ins Jesus had with the religious authorities.

Privately He taught His disciples that He would, in accordance with Scripture, suffer and die and rise from the dead (Luke 18:31–33). In fact later on, in speeches made by Peter, Stephen and Paul, all recorded by Dr Luke in the Acts of the Apostles, these events are repeatedly proclaimed as a fulfilment of God's promises. In other words, all of this is to be found in the Old Testament.

Leaders of many other religions were primarily endeavouring to find the truth as to why we exist on the face of the earth. They then attempted to attain not only religious insight but devotion to that truth. But Jesus Christ made it known that God was reaching down to those who are reaching up, and to others who weren't reaching anywhere. His offer was forgiveness, cleansing, a new heart and a new beginning. Most of those Christ and His early disciples spoke to were either fully absorbed or at least on the edges of religion.

Having overcome the onslaught of the devil Jesus called a group of men to follow Him, revealed something of His glory by changing water into wine and performed a number of other miracles. He began to teach what was to become revolutionary truth. He even brought salvation to a Samaritan, traditionally enemies of the non-

Samaritan Jews. He cast out demons, revealing His power over human bodies and spiritual diseases, even over life and death.

Mounting antagonism no doubt agitated those early disciples, but Jesus Christ refused to be frightened by those who acted as His enemies. There were only 6000 Pharisees led by the Rabbis. Reading the gospels you would be forgiven for thinking there were 600,000 of them! Every time revolutionary truth is taught, miracles are performed and the disenfranchised are empowered, the Pharisees pop up as though they are waiting in the wings.

## The great conflict

As Jesus' popularity grew among the masses of Galilee, perhaps reaching its peak at the feeding of the 5000, the Pharisees decided something had to be done.

So while Jesus was planning to make His disciples the foundational pillars of the church, religious leaders were planning something else—they were trying to trap Him and subsequently punish Him.

(Jesus) left Galilee and went into the region of Judea to the other side of the Jordan. Large crowds followed him and he healed them there.

Some Pharisees came to him to test him. They asked, 'Is it lawful for a man to divorce his wife for any and every reason?'

'Haven't you read,' he replied, 'that at the beginning the Creator "made them male and female", and said, "For this reason a man will leave his father and mother and be united to his wife, and the two will become one flesh"? So they are no longer two but one. Therefore what God has joined together, let man not separate.'

'Why then,' they asked, 'did Moses command that a man give his wife a certificate of divorce and send her away?'

Jesus replied, 'Moses permitted you to divorce your wives because your hearts were hard. But it was not this way from the beginning. I tell you that anyone who divorces his wife, except for marital unfaithfulness, and marries another woman commits adultery.'

The disciples said to him, 'If this is the situation between a husband and wife, it is better not to marry.'

Jesus replied, 'Not everyone can accept this word, but only those to whom it has been given. For some are eunuchs because they were born that way; others were made that way by men; and others have renounced marriage because of the kingdom of heaven. The one who can accept this should accept it.' (Matthew 19:1–12)

I suppose we should be thankful that the Pharisees drew out a great deal of wisdom and teaching that we would not otherwise have had from the lips of our Saviour. Nevertheless whilst Jesus was getting on shaping up His disciples for the decades that would follow His death, resurrection and ascension into heaven, He faced continual and often physical opposition. This came not from the godless, those on the edge of religion, but from those right at the heart of it. Yet He attended synagogue and knew the Scriptures well, gave generously and went around doing good. So He was seen as a good Jew, surely?

## Surely that is good religion?

Not so. Jesus' life, teaching and following were seen as a threat to the system, the religious system. The Jewish community was obliged to do certain things, but even in those days there were the committed and the lukewarm. But nobody was obliged to follow Jesus, walk for miles, spread the stories or receive whatever it was He had to give. But they followed Him by the thousand on occasion and thousands on others. So Jesus Christ became such a threat to the authority of the Pharisees and scribes that only His death would change things.

At times it seemed that Jesus deliberately enflamed the situation:

> Then some Pharisees and teachers of the law came to Jesus from Jerusalem and asked, 'Why do your disciples break the tradition of the elders? They don't wash their hands before they eat!'
>
> Jesus replied, 'And why do you break the command of God for the sake of your tradition? For God said "Honour your father and mother" and "Anyone who curses his father or mother must be put to death." But you say that if a man says to his father or mother, "Whatever help you might other-wise have received from me is a gift devoted to God," he is not to "honour his father" with it. Thus you nullify the word of God for the sake of your tradition. You hypocrites! Isaiah was right when he prophesied about you:
>
>> "These people honour me with their lips,
>>  but their hearts are far from me.

They worship me in vain;
    their teachings are but rules taught by men." '
        (Matthew 15:1–9)

Jesus went on to give further teaching when His disciples asked, 'Do you know that the Pharisees were offended when they heard this?' To which our Lord retorted, 'Leave them; they are blind guides. If a blind man leads a blind man, both will fall into a pit.' Peter didn't understand this at all and asked Jesus to explain. Our Lord responded, 'Are you still so dull?' He went on to explain what He meant (Matthew 15:12–16).

But Jesus didn't simply enflame the situation once, but apparently over and over again. Was this a matter of enough is enough? Righteous anger? Clarity amidst all the religious fog? Perhaps it was a mixture of all three.

Right there at the beginning of His ministry, having overcome the temptations of the devil, He returned to Galilee. News about him spread over the whole countryside. When He taught in synagogues everyone praised him.

One day He attended synagogue and read from the scroll of the prophet Isaiah. Explaining that this very day Scripture was being fulfilled, Luke records for us that 'All the people in the synagogue were furious when they heard this. They got up, drove him out of the town and took him to the brow of the hill on which the town was built, in order to throw him down the cliff' (Luke 4:28, 29).

## Deliberately offending?

Later on Dr Luke records that after Jesus had given a fine speech, a Pharisee invited Him to a meal. Although Dr

Luke doesn't say this, I am sure that the Pharisee was impressed with Jesus' teaching and wanted to discuss it with Him further. He then noticed that Jesus did not wash His hands before the meal and was somewhat surprised.

Suddenly, almost without warning it seems, Jesus launched into an attack:

> 'You Pharisees clean the outside of the cup and dish, but inside you are full of greed and wickedness . . . Woe to you Pharisees, because you give God a tenth of your mint, rue and all other kinds of garden herbs, but you neglect justice and the love of God . . . Woe to you Pharisees, because you love the most important seats in the synagogues and greetings in the market-places. Woe to you, because you are like unmarked graves, which men walk over without knowing it.' (Luke 11:37–44)

We shouldn't be surprised that one of the experts of the law commented, 'Teacher, when you say these things, you insult us also.' But Jesus replied, 'And you experts in the law, woe to you, because you load people down with burdens they can hardly carry and you yourselves will not lift one finger to help them.' And He goes on to another list of 'woe's!

And so 'the Pharisees and the teachers of the law began to oppose him fiercely and to besiege him with questions, waiting to catch him in something he might say' (Luke 11:45–53).

## So what is happening here?

God knows that shocking situations (that appear to be

nice and religious) often need to be addressed by shocking people in shocking language.

Even the most casual reading of the four gospels leads us to believe that the greatest threat to salvation reaching the ends of the earth did not come through atheists or agnostics, but from within the religious community to which Jesus belonged.

You would have thought religious leaders would have been the first to acknowledge Jesus Christ was the Messiah. They had Scripture, the miracles, the teaching and wisdom and more than three years to assess things. But they rejected His ministry and His theology simply because He offended their traditions and their ceremonies.

Pharisaism, both then and now, is acknowledging what God has done whilst resisting what God is doing.

Religion even in Jesus' day looked grand, impressive and created a sort of reverential awe. It was a powerful structure that looked unassailable. Leaders were the élite with special access to God. The rest were disadvantaged.

Perhaps it was then as it is today. Describe somebody as academic, very knowledgeable or 'theological' and though you may not agree with that person's perspectives, he or she is held in a certain respect, and regarded as superior. Describe someone as 'very emotional' and you will get the opposite response. Why is it that academic knowledge is valued above heart attitude, feelings, passion for justice and longing for better things?

To the religious leaders of Jesus' day religion became a purely intellectual and theological exercise. Hypocrisy, legalism and theological nit-picking were their very reason for existence. It would not be unfair to say—and Jesus made this clear—that the Pharisees greatly overplayed the role of theology. William De Arteaga points out in his excellent book *Quenching the Spirit:*

It will be fair to say that the main issue of contention between Jesus and the Pharisees was the relationship between the Torah (the first five books of the Bible) and the Talmud (the Pharisees' theological commentaries). In a broad sense the Torah represented the inspired word of God while the Talmud referred to theological commentaries.[3]

Religious leaders valued the Talmud as of equal importance to the Torah, whereas Jesus held no such conviction. God's law is eternal—both those ten commandments and the first five books of Scripture. Our interpretation may be helpful but can be dispensed with. So it is today, as we shall see.

It could be said that Jesus went around violating tradition and ceremony both frequently and purposefully.

## Sectarian interests

De Arteaga also points out that religious leaders in Jesus' day (and perhaps today) do not mind people doing things providing it is in their name or in the name of their denomination. But when Peter and John were used to heal a lame man, the response of the Pharisees was 'By what power or what name did you do this?' The fact that a man had been healed was of little importance to them, but who they represented *was* of significant importance. They soon realised that these men 'had been with Jesus'. This was not a sloppy, sentimental observation because they had unruffled personalities and spoke with a lilting accent. They were nigh terrified! One Jesus was enough, but now there were three, how many more would there be? They held a consultation in camera. 'Everybody living in Jerusalem knows that they have done an outstanding miracle and we cannot deny it. But to stop this thing from spreading any further among the people, we must warn these men to speak no longer to anyone in this name.' In other words just as it was then, so it is today, that those of us who see signs and wonders outside our own circle can often get threatened for no other reason than that they do not come from a traditional school of thought or theology.

Jesus did not demean theological expertise. He knew His Bible well, and it could be rightly argued that it was from Scripture He found His identity. He certainly quoted Scripture to His disciples and to others to validate who He was and why He was doing what He was doing. On the day of Pentecost Peter, one of the three on the inner circle of His original twelve, quoted Scripture to explain what was happening that day. Both the speaker and the listeners must have known Scripture to have any understanding whatever of what was going on. There is no virtue in an empty head. Yet it seems that that is not where Jesus placed the emphasis of His ministry. This cannot be stressed sufficiently.

Discipleship in Jesus' day was casting out demons, healing the sick, identifying with the powerless, laying one's life down for one's friends and even those who are not of the household of faith. How different today. Discipleship is going to university, then Bible college and getting into a form of ministry where one's contact with the unbelieving world is minimal. There are of course some notable exceptions—those who have been through university and Bible college who then go into the teaching profession or social services. But that is not the route most church leaders take.

Discipleship therefore becomes an issue of

knowledge, academic learning, memorising the Bible. It is not that these things are bad within themselves. I cannot underline that sufficiently. Our Lord studied the scriptures and memorised them. Two people were on their way to Emmaus when Jesus came up and started walking with them. As they talked about events that had taken place, including Christ's death, Jesus responded, 'Beginning with Moses and all the prophets he (Jesus) explained to them what was said in all the scriptures concerning himself.' Pressing Him to stay with them overnight they had a meal together and Jesus broke bread with them. He disappeared from their sight. They turned to each other, asking, 'Were not our hearts burning within us while he talked with us on the road and opened the scriptures to us?' (Luke 24:13–32). This incident helps us understand that those who are not able to see can be helped to see. Those who do not understand can be helped to understand, particularly through Scripture. But those who claim that the work of the Holy Spirit is really the activity of demons are not simply in trouble—it is in fact unforgivable. It is saying that Christian leaders and churches are involved in sorcery.

The Pharisees decided to remove the sorcerer by telling lies about Him. Yet they were the ones who seemed to be most interested in truth. They were not interested in truth, simply theological rectitude—and there is a difference.

It was not the truth they were interested in, but their interpretation of the truth. To listen to some church leaders in the latter years of the twentieth century, particularly those from the Reformed camp, you could be forgiven for thinking they believed that the church disappeared after a century or so and only reappeared again 400 years ago, at the Reformation! Their bookshelves explain this most adequately, as do their sermons.

What you will not hear from many Christian leaders today is that God the Holy Spirit and the word of God were active for one and a half millennia, before Calvin, Luther, Zwingli and their colleagues.

But because the Holy Spirit used people who did not come from their camp, or see things their way, they may as well all have been torn from the pages of church history. But these men and women were not cessationists (believing that the gifts of the Holy Spirit are no longer active today). They believed in the power of the Spirit as well as the word of God. Many church leaders today barely mention the colossal revivals going on in South America, Africa, parts of Eastern Europe, China and the Philippines. Why?  Because virtually all are related to prayer and intercession (with which they would agree) but also signs and wonders, miracles, apostolic and prophetic ministry—which Reformed, conservative cessationists do not believe in.

It should also be noted the vast majority of Christians throughout the world, particularly in the nations I have mentioned, have never heard of Calvin or Luther, Zwingli or their crowd. It would be unfair to say that these men were without significance and import during a time of apostasy, indulgences and heresy. They and many of their followers paid a great price for the gospel.

But the issues facing us in these latter years of the twentieth century bare little resemblance to the issues of the sixteenth century. Most of those Calvin was endeavouring to influence were already regarded as churched. Today the vast majority of people in the Western world are not only not in church, they are unchurched and barely know the basic facts of Jesus' birth, life, death and resurrection.

So we need to view modern-day and historical church

figures through Jesus Christ. We must not view Jesus Christ through the church fathers.

## Jesus' true opponents

Jesus was honoured by the masses; they wanted to crown Him. Jesus refused that crown. But He forgave their sins, healed their diseases and delivered them from demonic forces. He had few opponents among such people.

The main opponents were orthodox, conservative 'believers'. Though there were only 6000 of them, the Pharisees were committed to their view of Scripture, devout in prayers and unlike the Sadducees (who concentrated on temple-centred worship), they committed themselves to synagogues. Through it they won the support, though not necessarily the goodwill, of many people.

Leaders among the Pharisees were scribes, later called Rabbis. Most were not 'full time'. The astounding thing is, that they could be expelled from the group simply for nonconformity.

We should never forget that criticism of the Pharisees came from Jesus, not only His followers or later apostles. When He called them hypocrites He referred to the fact that they were merely acting rather than deceiving or pretending. In other words they were fulfilling a role. Failure to fulfil the role meant expulsion from the group.

My friend R. T. Kendall, a Reformed theologian and Bible teacher, has experienced just that. Now filling the famous pulpit at Westminster Chapel, he told me, 'You are more acceptable to my Reformed colleagues than I am—you were never one of them!' And yet Dr Kendall has a greater heart for the lost than many I know, is out on the streets most Saturdays witnessing in his own territory, gives what many would regard to be some of the finest exegesis of Scripture around and lives as far as I know a moral life, based upon a strong family relationship. But many of his Reformed friends are not remotely interested in those aspects of his life or ministry. He has departed from theological acceptability and that is regarded by many as worse than adultery or telling lies.

So far we have dealt with religion as it emerged in the Old Testament, albeit in headline form, and as a kind of précis. We have also looked at the opposition the Lord Jesus Christ faced as He endeavoured to bring the very Spirit of heaven to the earth. It was through orthodox, religious leaders.

Apart from my own inadequacy in taking hold of such lofty and complex issues both in the Old Testament and Jesus' ministry, I imagine that most of my readers will given a knowing nod of agreement to most of what I have written. It is there, plain for all to see and the only areas of caution may be in my emphasis and what I have chosen to include or exclude in making the point. But the real issue is where the rubber hits the road in daily life, as we move towards the year 2000. Other than God and His word nothing is sacred.

So here goes!

# CHAPTER 3

# SCAFFOLDING AND BUILDING

Scaffolding in the building trade is simply called 'temporary works'. In fact, builders have told me that when they are doing a job on, say, a house, they might order '2000 metres of temporary works'.

The scaffolding is vital to get a job done. But no builder would ever confuse the scaffolding with the building. One would assume, after scaffolding has gone up around the Houses of Parliament in London or a bungalow in Bournemouth, offices in Birmingham or a church building in Dundee, that when they were dismantled a job will have been done.

That job may be to clean up the tons of grime that gather on the Palace of Westminster. It may be to put a new roof on the bungalow. It could be to replace window frames in the offices or to repair serious cracks in the church building. But temporary works, scaffolding, is for a purpose.

I can attend church buildings, take communion, engage in the gospel meeting, the prayer meeting, Sunday schools, Bible classes, door-to-door work, youth clubs, choirs, leadership itself, but all are temporary works, to get a job done.

In other words ministry, Ephesians 4 ministry, is here to produce the church. The church is not here simply to produce Ephesians 4 ministries.

Scaffolding is here to get something built which will

make Christ attractive and intelligible to those around us, so that they will be added to those whose eternal destiny will be heaven. The primary purpose of that community is not to create more scaffolding or Ephesians 4 ministry.

But the main problem emerges when scaffolding, temporary works, things provided to get a job done, become permanent. So today we have ecclesiastical scaffolding, gold-plated scaffolding, charismatic scaffolding, seeker-sensitive scaffolding, nonconformist scaffolding—in fact much of it has been up for so long it is virtually impossible to dismantle it. Old and rusty, it sometimes has to be left behind to erect new scaffolding, to start on a new site.

Suggest to the average evangelical church that instead of having a 'nip and a sip' on a Sunday morning (without even talking to each other!) they break bread at home. You will probably have the equivalent of a third world war on your hands. Yet Scripture is clear that the breaking of bread took place primarily in homes. Church buildings were not in common usage until around the fourth century.

Suggest that Sunday school attended exclusively by children of church members disbands and that the children should be looked after by their parents. You will find in many the deep impression that the church is there to look after their children. In my own church, we are taught that parents are there to look after their children and anything the church does is a bonus.

Suggest that the 6.30 gospel meeting makes way for something else. I can still hear the cries of 'But what if someone unchurched comes in?' In the church I came from nobody ever came in! Even if they did the language was almost incomprehensible. People spoke in a language the unchurched wouldn't understand, referring to biblical types, metaphors and illustrations they had never heard of.

## Touching the scaffolding

One Spirit-filled evangelical vicar I know decided to abolish the choir. It was costing thousands upon thousands of pounds a year. A number of those in the choir had no commitment whatever to the local church nor to his leadership. When, after a process of discussion and dialogue, its demise was agreed, it got into the local press, national press and there were letters of complaint to the Bishop. All this at a time when bishops were denying the Virgin birth, the uniqueness of Christ's salvation and the resurrection. Don't touch the scaffolding—it is eternal. But you can change the church's message—it is only temporary.

In my book *Kingdom Now!* I wrote, 'Of course He (Jesus) did not go out of His way to deliberately offend; He had better things to do than that.'[1]

But two years later I am not so sure.

Jesus Christ fully understood what God's original intention was in the garden of Eden, why God chose an individual (Adam), a family (Noah's) and then the man called Abraham who was to bless a generation and then generations. He also understood that God in His mercy gave the law, prophets, priests and kings to provide safety, health and focus in the here and now and to provide hope for a better future.

But He also knew that other than the word of God, which is eternal and unchanging, everything else was temporary works. Through the re-reading of Scripture I have come to realise that Jesus had much more strategy

1   Gerald Coates, *Kingdom Now!* (Kingsway, 1993), page 48.

in what He was doing than I formerly realised. He seemed on occasion to target those who thought they were protectors of orthodoxy and the nation's values, when in fact they were actually opponents of the Holy Spirit.

We live in an age where excitement is mistaken for mindless enthusiasm. But Jesus Christ seemed positively enthusiastic, passionate and emotional in His criticism, as we have seen in the previous chapter.

Scaffolding, temporary works, can be the God-given means to achieve an end. On the other hand it can merely be a tradition or a collection of traditions, which have little relevance other than to a minority, who are consumed with them.

Tradition, quite simply, is that which is handed down. This is particularly true of teaching, handed down from a teacher to a disciple.

Strangely enough the word does not occur in the Old Testament. But nevertheless, as we have seen, things handed down orally, as well as in written form, assumed an authority similar if not identical to that of Scripture. The matching of human commentary with divine revelation was condemned by Christ. Eugene H. Peterson has done us all a great favour with his New Testament in contemporary English, *The Message*. This is how he interprets the opening verses of the fifteenth chapter of Matthew:

> After that Pharisees and religious scholars came to Jesus all the way from Jerusalem, criticising, 'Why do your disciples play fast and loose with the rules?' But Jesus put it right back on them: 'Why do you use your rules to play fast and loose with God's commands? God clearly says, "Respect your father and mother," and, "Anyone denouncing father or mother should be killed." But you weasel around

that by saying, "Whoever wants to can say to father and mother, 'What I owed to you I have given to God.' " That can hardly be called respecting a parent. You cancel God's command by your rules. Frauds! Isaiah's prophecy of you hit the bull's-eye: "These people make a big show of saying the right thing but their heart isn't in it. They act as if they are worshipping me but they don't mean it. They just use me as a cover for teaching whatever suits their fancy." '

Dealing with the issues of heart, Jesus addresses Peter who isn't getting the message. 'Are you being wilfully stupid? Don't you know that anything that is swallowed works its way through the intestines and is finally defecated. But what comes out of the mouth gets its start in the heart. It is from the heart that we vomit up evil arguments, murders, adulteries, fornications, thefts, lies and cursing. That is what pollutes. Eating or not eating certain foods, washing and not washing your hands—that is neither here nor there.'

The word 'tradition' is used in the gospels but only Jewish tradition. Jesus did in fact place His own teaching alongside the word of God as an authoritative commentary. He then handed that down to His disciples. In the Sermon on the Mount Jesus quotes the law, and then adds 'but I say unto you' (Matthew 5:22, 28, 32, 34, 39, AV). But Jesus claimed He was fulfilling the law, not disempowering it.

Staying with Eugene Peterson's interpretation for a while, this is how we read Paul on the issue:

My counsel for you is simple and straightforward: just go ahead with what you have been given. You received Christ Jesus the master; now live Him. You are deeply rooted in Him. You are well constructed upon Him. You know your way around the faith. Now do what you have been taught. School's out; quit studying the subject and start living it! And let your living spill over into thanksgiving.

Watch out for people who try to dazzle you with big words and intellectual double talk. They want to drag you off into endless arguments that never amount to anything. They spread their ideas through the empty traditions of human beings and the empty superstitions of spirit beings. But that is not the way of Christ. Everything of God gets expressed in Him, so you can see and hear Him clearly. You don't need a telescope, a microscope or a horoscope to realise the fullness of Christ and the emptiness of the universe without Him. When you come to Him the fullness comes together for you too. His power extends over everything (Colossians 2:7–10).

So the contrast to human tradition and at times even Jewish tradition is Jesus Christ. Christ is the true tradition.


## Perception and reality

So we as Christians, and particularly those in places of influence, have to be continually assessing what is scaffolding and what is building—what may be God-given means to get a job done and what is merely tradition. This can cut very deeply not only into church structures but into personal taste on a wide range of issues.

The vicar of a large Anglican church decided to make his building user-friendly. Knowing the building as it was, I was astonished when some months later I returned to find that the unattractive pews had been ripped out, tasteful carpet been laid, attractive and comfortable chairs had replaced the pews and the most exquisite redecoration had gone on, bringing the old building up to date but without violating the design and architecture. Stained glass windows remained, as did mosaics and tablets commemorating the dead (personally, I would have taken these out!). My wife, with a background in interior design and display, and I concluded that it would be difficult to improve upon what they had done.

But when the Bishop and his wife came to view the building prior to an evening to celebrate the refurbishment, she was appalled. In fact she was so appalled she stomped out of the church building and sat in the car park, while the vicar conducted the Bishop around the building showing him what had been done and why. Her disgrace and disgust continued over into the next day. That night the Bishop was present when around 1000 members of the congregation came to the church building to give thanks for the refurbished building. She pointedly refused to come. The mayor and his wife were present, so were the vicar and his wife. But there was an empty chair for the Bishop's wife. The evening was yet again a remarkable blend of the old and the new, with a brilliant classical pianist from former Yugoslavia, a soft rock five-piece band, hymns and modern songs. Old and young were involved.

But the Bishop's wife seemed uninterested in the hundreds of people who had come to Christ in that church over the previous few years, nor a similar number who had been baptised in the Spirit; nor in the many evangelistic initiatives that have spawned churches or those who had been in a backslidden state who have come back to Christ, found faith and are today being useful in the Kingdom. All she saw was traditional pews removed, the traditional wooden and tiled floor carpeted over, the 'reverential' atmosphere overtaken by chumminess and mateyness.

Of course much of what goes for reverence has got nothing to do with a scriptural view of reverence. It is merely tradition that causes people to creep around, trying not to make a noise. One could argue that putting a carpet down would alleviate the necessity to mimic John Cleese and his ministry of funny walks in church on a Sunday morning.

But it is much easier to see the speck or plank in others than it is to recognise it in our own life and church.

## Nearer to home

One Sunday morning I had a fairly well-known singer from another country come and do a presentation at Esher Cinema, which is where our church is currently meeting. After two or three carols and readings our guest did about an hour or more of songs and commentary regarding the meaning of Christmas. Afterwards the feedback was nothing short of amazing. 'Sentimental rubbish,' one called it. Another said, 'Unbelievably awful' and another 'Shouldn't have been in the main meeting, should have been a special evangelistic event for those who wanted to go.' It was in fact a main talking point for some days for quite a few in the church.

What they didn't focus on was that we had the largest attendance of unconverted people at the cinema ever. We also had a significant number of people who are married to members of our church who have not been in any sort of meeting for at least a year or even two. One of them made his way back to Christ publicly and the others began a journey back to Christ. Gospel literature was given out, seeds were sown and prayers were made for specific people at their request!  But all of that was of no interest to people who only wanted to let others know that the singer was not to their personal taste. There was an unwillingness to lay aside musical preference, traditional modern songs and a traditional liturgy for a charismatic New Church.  Those criticising the morning were quite happy for the singer to be hived off to a specialist event, which by implication tends to be by invitation only. It was of little relevance to them that people walked in, quite literally off the street, as the result of reading about the morning in the local press or through some special leaflets that were handed out.

We can sing about taking the land for Jesus, marching upon the land, we can pray for revival and a massive move of God's Spirit across our area, but we don't want to be inconvenienced. We don't want it to upset our traditional approach to worship, teaching and ministry. We all have liturgy and the most dangerous are those who suggest they haven't got one!

Having been brought up in the Plymouth Brethren, I know how much we used to laugh at our Anglican friends (but they weren't friends really) with their hymn prayer sandwich, stand-up, kneel-down approach to things. But if any of our Anglican friends had come to our breaking of bread service on a Sunday morning they would have found a strict start time, a strict finish time, the actual breaking of bread taking place almost 50 minutes after the start, week after week. And we thought we had no tradition.

I well remember the morning when John, in a state of nervousness, gave thanks for the wine first and passed it round, and then the bread. Nobody stopped him in the meeting, and as it was a Sunday morning some of us were too tired to notice that he had the order round the wrong way. But afterwards you would have thought he had propositioned one of the elder's wives for sex! It was unbelievable.

It has long been a conviction of mine that although Protestant churches, from Anglican right the way through to the New Churches, emphasise that bread and wine are only symbols, they do not actually believe that. Every Sunday morning in our Brethren assembly one could hear:

> Only bread and only wine
> Yet to faith the solemn sign
> Of the heavenly and divine.

The somewhat clumsy doggerel nevertheless makes one thing clear. What we have on this table is simply bread and wine. But to our faith it is a sign of something much deeper—the bread signifying the body of our Lord, broken for us and the wine, blood that was shed for us. In other words we do not believe in transubstantiation. We do not believe that bread and wine actually become something else. In that sense the emblems and symbols do not become holy. They are simply bread and wine. When Jesus first took bread and encouraged His disciples to remember Him in the breaking of the bread and the drinking of the cup, He actually took bread they were already eating and wine they were already drinking. It was a special meal to be sure, but the Jewish community were under no illusion as to what the bread and wine was or was to become.

## Symbols or holy things?

I have often told the story which is worth repeating. While I was in New Zealand with my friend and colleague Noel Richards, we spoke at a charismatic evangelical conference on the themes of worship, prayer and evangelism. If you think the British are conservative, go to New Zealand! But by the end of the few days relationships had been formed and there was a great freedom in worship, and response to the teaching.

On the final night—a Saturday—that freedom extended to some people standing on their chairs with their arms in the air worshipping, with tears running down their faces. Then came Sunday morning. I arrived, as I am prone to, just before the meeting started. I love to hang around after a meeting, talking and praying with people and getting their feedback. But I don't like arriving early and getting too involved in discussions and sometimes differences of opinion, prior to speaking to a large group.

As I walked in I could hear Noel saying, 'He won't like this.' The 'this' was a long table covered in bread and thimbles full of wine. The reasons for his comments will become apparent.

Looking round the conference room you could hardly believe that this group, now all in suits, shirts and ties, or smart dresses, were the same group who were shouting, clapping, laughing and crying, some standing on their chairs, the night before. The effect of a table full of bread and blackcurrant juice was colossal. It had killed the thing stone dead. The atmosphere was as flat as a pancake. One could be forgiven for feeling that God had died overnight. Noel led worship—it was like walking through treacle. The subject I had prepared was inappropriate. Pulling a large cloth which looked like a curtain off the table, I pointed to the bread and wine: 'This is the worst meeting you know in the church calendar.' I went on to speak of pretence, false reverential fear, a communion where we were neither communing with one another nor, in my experience, with God. We are thinking rather than thanking. This has little to do with what goes on before the meeting and it has little to do with what will go on over lunch. It is a religious exercise where everybody is mega sincere, and that is about it. It has little to do with the context of Passover or the Lord's Supper in the early church. That was in the context of a meal, with friends, where they talked to each other as well as their Lord.

I then took a piece of bread and began to eat it. People walked out. 'Why are you leaving?' I enquired. 'We are all going to have some bread in a moment—I am just having mine early!' More people walked out. Eventually I got people up and sent them round to one another to break bread, pray with each other and to create interaction and reality. But it was quite clear that there were those present who thought my actions were full of disrespect and I was being irreligious. There is a difference between nonreligious and irreligious just as there is a difference between non-Christian and anti-Christian.

I often wonder what would Jesus do if He came to one of our meetings? How would He act and respond to our Sunday mornings with our wafers and Ribena? The gospel on a Sunday evening to the converted? Or indeed in many churches, including charismatic evangelical churches, the complete lack of a gospel presentation and any meeting whatever, other than something specialist, hived away for the interested and committed.

## Heart, not cosmetic

Religious people perform superficially what only Christ

can change fundamentally. Christianity has little to do with meeting the standards of superficial behaviour. Religious people, and religious churches, cut themselves off from reality.

I may be charged with cutting the Pioneer network of churches off from our theological and historical roots. I want to respond by saying, 'No, I am going back to them'. We should not forget that most church life took place in homes, not special buildings, led by people in regular clothes, not dog collars, never mind robes. The synagogues were primarily used to debate and dialogue the nature of salvation. But Jesus and most of His disciples were eventually thrown out.

There are times when I ridicule the church because it is ridiculous. We speakers and writers must nevertheless pay as much attention to what we are saying as we want our listeners to. We rarely see how ridiculous we or our own churches are. Religious people are not religious simply because they do things differently from us, whether it is singing from a book, reading from a different Bible version or conducting their meetings with candles and vestments in special buildings. The religious spirit is something much deeper than that. As I read Scripture, I have come to some very firm conclusions about the nature of church. There is a lot of paraphernalia which has little or nothing to do with simplicity of the gospel or church life. But we mustn't imagine that because people meet in special buildings and do things differently from ourselves, they are religious.

The awful and terrible thing is that you can meet in a school hall with none of the outward symbols one associates with religiosity, and you can be as religious as hell. It is a matter of the heart. As Joel prophesied, 'Rend your heart and not your garments. Return to the Lord your God, for he is gracious and compassionate, slow to anger and abounding in love, and he relents from sending calamity (Joel 2:13). We test the value of something by its fruit. What is all this producing, we have to ask ourselves? Recently we closed down almost everything in our church for a season of intimacy and togetherness. We have a plethora of meetings, layer upon layer of forums and planning events and at the end of it all I have to ask—what fruit is this bearing? What is it producing? Are we just driven by activity, meetings and diaried commitments? That season of intimacy, where we met as a church three evenings a week as well as Sunday mornings, over a period of months, allowed us to reassess the fruitfulness of our work and ways.

We have looked at how religion emerged in the Old Testament, how Christ confronted religion and how it confronted Him in the New Testament. In this chapter through anecdotes and Scripture we have looked at where the rubber hits the road. Those looking for understanding and ideas will probably have appreciated the first two chapters more than this one. Those looking for a practical approach to Christianity may have dutifully waded through the first two chapters to get to this one. But the former without the latter means we have ideas which do not engage with reality. The latter without the former means we may be nearer to Christ in the way we live as well as in our usefulness, but we may not know why. That will make it difficult to articulate our faith to others.

It is so easy to slip back from God's grace into a new form of law, legislation and legalism. The snare is, it is difficult to recognise in the short term. The fact is that we are all incredibly religious at heart. How does that happen?

# CHAPTER 4

# RELIGIOUS LAWS AND GOD'S GRACE

It is easy for us as Christians to live in a self-sustaining world, fulfilling objectives, almost without any reference to Christ. We set an attainable goal, meet it and that is how you become self-righteous.

Others of us set a goal, don't meet it and have to cover up. At heart we feel we are failures, unholy, unclean and become ashamed and disappointed. Most people end up under some form of religious law, because initially they want to please God and want His approval.

If the powers of darkness cannot keep us from the gospel and from making a response, they have another strategy. That is, to convey that God is something other than who He really is; that His character and nature are different from what the devil knows Him to be.

Every letter Paul wrote he begins with 'the grace of God' and finishes with 'the grace of God'. He never got over the grace of God. To Paul sin was no longer an inevitability for the Christian—simply a possibility. He was not unaware of the need for confession and repentance, to acknowledge he got things wrong. He changed plans and personnel. He was free.

But what have we been set free for? True, we have been set free from sin, though we have not been set free from pain. But we have also been set free from working hard to merit divine favour. So I come back to my question. It is not so much *from what* have we been set free, but *why* have we been set free?

'It is for freedom that Christ has set us free,' exclaimed the Apostle Paul. He then went on to explain that we should 'stand firm' in that freedom and 'not let [our-]selves be burdened again by a yoke of slavery' (Galatians 5:1).

When we read the New Testament it is not long before we realise that the Apostle Paul and the apostolic teams and councils often faced serious problems. Racism, sexism and nationalism were not far from their concerns. What was the principle on which they endeavoured to unify morality and tradition in the churches?

All of us lean towards legalism or licence. It may surprise you that Jesus, the Apostle Paul and those early church councils always leaned in the direction of freedom, liberty and, one could say inevitably, licence. The biggest issue facing the early church was the issue of Jewish believers relating to Gentiles. The Jews believed that they were inheritors by divine providence. How could they relate to non-Jews, the Gentiles, who had largely been brought up without Scripture, without any understanding of the ways of God? The big issue was how much of the Jewish tradition should be placed upon the non-Jews.

The church was, initially exclusively, and over a time primarily, made up of born-again Jews. They still went to the synagogue, celebrated the Jewish festivals and by implication were following religious leaders who were not born again. Most of these actually rejected the Messiah. Even when the born again were thrown out of the synagogues or pulled away from those religious frameworks, they were still Jews, with all the ceremony and tradition that made a person a proper believing Jew.

# Gentile Jews?

But what about the Gentiles? Should they be asked to refrain from eating pork? Or should they be required to wash their hands and cooking utensils in a certain way? Should they be expected to go only so far on a Sabbath journey? There were, as we have already noted, over 600 laws—to break one simply meant you were a law breaker. You either keep the whole law or break it. It should be remembered that these were not simply theoretical ideas—the apostles were dealing with grass-root issues.

It is not dissimilar to the Vegetarian Society being asked to live alongside the beef industry. It makes eating together rather difficult. And as much Jewish life centred around the meal table, the issue of what to eat, how and when was a crucial one.

'Everything is permissible'—but not everything is beneficial. 'Everything is permissible'—but not everything is constructive. Nobody should seek his own good, but the good of others.

Eat anything sold in the meat market without raising questions of conscience, for, 'The earth is the Lord's and everything in it.'

If some unbeliever invites you to a meal and you want to go, eat whatever is put before you without raising questions of conscience. But if anyone says to you, 'This has been offered in sacrifice,' then do not eat it, both for the sake of the man who told you and for conscience' sake—the other man's conscience, I mean, not yours. For why should my freedom by judged by another's conscience? If I take part in the meal with thankfulness, why am I denounced because of something I thank God for?

So whether you eat or drink or whatever you

do, do it all to the glory of God. Do not cause anyone to stumble, whether Jews, Greeks or the church
of God—even as I try to please everybody in every
way. For I am not seeking my own good but the
good of many, so that they may be saved. Follow
my example, as I follow the example of Christ'
(1 Corinthians 10:23—11:1).

In a separate incident Paul and Barnabas met with
apostles and elders in Jerusalem to deal with the issue of
Jewish and Gentile believers, their morals and their
behaviour. After a great deal of debate which involved
Peter and James they came to a number of conclusions.
They then conveyed those conclusions and judgements in
a letter to the church in Antioch.
    Explaining that they had heard that visiting preachers
had, without their authority, troubled the church in
Antioch, they then explained they were sending Judas
and Silas. This was the message they took.

It seemed good to the Holy Spirit and to us not to
burden you with anything beyond the following
requirements: you are to abstain from food sacri-
ficed to idols, from blood, from the meat of
strangled animals and from sexual immorality. You
will do well to avoid these things (Acts 15:28–9).

These, it appears, were the minimum requirements
and at the same time the only requirements  the apostles
and elders were going to put on a large church such as
Antioch. They were keen to put as few 'requirements' on
them as possible. Abstaining from sexual immorality is
almost put on the same level as not eating meat which
has been strangled!  One could easily detect that they
didn't want to put any restrictions on the church at all,

but for the sake of unbelievers, and particularly Gentiles, this was necessary to help them come to faith. In other words they did not err on the side of law, legalism, rules and regulations. They erred on the side of grace and  the licence that can come from that grace.

They could have put many more requirements on the church, to keep things safe, to hedge the church in to keep them from sin, but they chose not to do so. This is a major emphasis in all of Paul's teaching to the churches across Galatia, in the church in Rome and Colossae, in particular.

How unlike many of the religious leaders of the day, whom Jesus Christ castigated for the colossal gap between what they taught and how they lived.

The religious scholars and Pharisees are competent teachers of God's law. You won't go wrong in following their teaching on Moses. But be careful about following them. They talk a good line, but they don't live it. They don't take it into their hearts and live it out in their behaviour. It is all spit and polish veneer. Instead of giving you God's Law as food and drink by which you can banquet on God, they package it in bundles of rules, loading you down like packed animals. They seem to take pleasure in watching you stagger under these loads, and wouldn't think of lifting a finger to help. Their lives are perpetual fashion shows, embroidered prayer shawls one day and flowery prayers the next. They love to sit at the head of the table at church dinners, basking in the most prominent positions, preening in the radiance of public flattery, receiving honorary degrees and getting called 'Doctor' and 'Reverend'.[1]

---

1  Matthew 23:1–7 in E. H. Peterson, *The Message* (NavPress, 1993).

And stepping on a few more toes, if not driving a steam roller across feet that happen to get into the way, he adds:

> Don't set people up as experts over your life, letting them tell you what to do. Save that authority for God; let Him tell you what to do. No one else should carry the title of 'father'; you have only one father and He is in heaven. And don't let people manoeuvre you into taking charge of them. There is only one Life-Leader for you and them—Christ. In doubt?  Then step down, be a servant. If you puff yourself up, you get the wind knocked out of you. But if you are content to simply be yourself, your life will count for plenty.[2]

The point of all this is that we were not made for burdens, but for freedom. We were not made for religious structures, but for intimacy with God and one another. Fulfilled burdens can puff us up, giving us an air of superiority because we are doing well. Unfulfilled burdens create a climate for pretence. It was Sir Laurence Olivier who said, 'I am never happier than when I am being someone else other than myself.'  Many Christians who feel exactly the same are trapped in churches. They are living out someone else's fantasies or their own fantasies as to what a Christian should be, how they should behave—they are simply spending their lives spinning plates.

## Purpose and freedom

But once we are free, truly free and understand the nature

---

2  Matthew 23:8–14 in *The Message*.

of freedom we then have to ask what we are going to do with that freedom. Of course one cannot have freedom without responsibility. In the apocryphal story of the man walking down a High Street pavement swinging his arms around, he hits a passer-by. 'What do you think you are doing?' the bruised pedestrian enquires, somewhat angrily. 'I am free, I am free, I am free!' the arm-flailing man responds. As quick as a flash the other man, nursing his bruise, retorts, 'Your freedom stops where my face starts!'

So you either live by rules and laws for yourself and for others, or you choose to live responsibly with your freedom. But the end result seems the same. I understand that argument. If God looks upon the heart, however, He knows that much of what we do has got nothing to do with our heart, loyalties and affections. It has to do with pleasing the crowd, or gratifying a demanding God.

Confusion came in part because Jesus said that He came to fulfil the law rather than abolish it (Matthew 5:17). But we should remember that the new covenant, the new agreement God has with His people, did not come into place until after Calvary and the resurrection. Jesus lived under the old covenant, and He came to fulfil the Ten Commandments, but more importantly the law of love.

The Ten Commandments and the law in general can be summed up in one word—respect. Respect for God, for the devil, for yourself, your friends, your enemies and the world around you. Fail to show respect in any of those areas and you sin against God or His people or both.

## Another spirit

On the day of Pentecost when Jesus breathed on His

disciples, He filled them with another spirit. It was the promise of the father, it was the spirit of promise. Whereas the law demanded, 'You shall have no other gods before me' (Exodus 20:3), when the spirit of promise was given commands yielded to hope. The promise is 'You shall have no other gods before me.' It is a promise. We are children of promise. We respond to a promise by saying, 'Thank you Father, I will put no other gods before you. I will not commit adultery, thank you!  I will not steal, thank you! I will not lie, thank you!'

We are not fulfilling a list of rules. When the spirit of promise came, the promise was you will not do these things. And all the time we walk in faith, embracing the promise of God, conscious of His presence, we fulfil the promises.

This sort of Christianity is infectious, it is generous, it is full of grace and mercy. It allows others to be different from us; it allows other churches to create different models and be different from our own. It means we have less to criticise because in the final analysis we are asking important questions about the fruit in people's lives, our effectiveness in reaching out to the lost and the quality of life that allows us to be signs and symbols. In previous ages holy things were wrapped up in religious paraphernalia. Today we don't need many signs and symbols—we are the signs and symbols!

What this means is that the whole of life is to be lived for the Lord. No sacred/secular compartments—there are no special holy buildings, special holy places, special holy vestments, special holy dates—the whole of life is holy. Every day is the Lord's, every building we own should be given to Him. Every item of our apparel should give glory to God.

Of course one honours the architects of vast cathedrals. We can enjoy Christmas and the vestiges that are left of our Sundays. They are a part of the cultural baggage of our time and we should be free to enjoy them, not merely endure them; but they are not vital to Christianity. Along with our modern-day baggage we face a number of other issues. Take women's ordination. *Christianity Today*, the fine, conservative evangelical magazine published in the USA, interviewed me about the issue. 'Are you concerned about the women the Church of England are about to ordain?' they asked. 'Not nearly as much as I am about most of the men they have ordained already!' I replied. 'I can think of many reasons for leaving the Church of England, but recognising women in leadership and ministry is not one of them. It is bizarre.'

We have got vicars having sex with male members of their own congregation, we have bishops denying core values and creedal statements of the historic orthodox faith, we have people who deny the need for the new birth and even the historical authenticity of Jesus Christ. I know that, because I have talked to these people. We are told the Church of England is a large pool 'in which one can fish'. But along comes recognition for women in leadership and ministry and people go and join the Roman Catholic church! In that religion they virtually worship and adore a woman!

It is true that women in special outfits and collars turned around the wrong way look ridiculous. But so do men in ecclesiastical robes. I happen to think they suit women better than men.


## God's blessing isn't respectable

We also have what the national press have called 'The Toronto Blessing'. Most readers will be aware that in

January 1994 Randy Clark visited the Vineyard church at the end of the runway in Toronto and the pastor, John Arnott, recognised that this was a special visitation from God. Since then they have been meeting in their most improbable church building every night, Mondays aside. Tens of thousands of people have been personally renewed and revived. They have gone back to their churches and brought the blessing to their local church. To date almost 5000 churches in the UK, well over a tenth, have experienced 'times of refreshing', this move of God, this outpouring of the Holy Spirit. Notwithstanding the pastoral issues this sort of thing throws up, with people on the floor laughing, crying, shaking and doing all sorts of other quite strange things, leaders, leadership teams and churches have been completely revolutionised. They have got a passion back for Christ, for Scripture, for prayer, and there is a desire to be together and to go out and reach the lost.

And yet the Pharisees, because that is what they are, have criticised the movement because 'These things are not in the Bible.' My first response is they don't know their Bibles very well, or they are selective in the parts they take seriously.

Many Christian leaders have a completely unbiblical approach to the Bible. It is not given as a text book but as a test book. We are not looking for a proof text for everything we do, but we should bring our lives up against Scripture and test them accordingly.

The sick man had no Bible text, putting himself in the shadow of Peter to get healed, but it didn't stop him getting healed! There was a wide range of behaviour in the early church for which there were no texts—they just seemed the sensible and right thing to do in the light of the broad teaching of Scripture.

In my latest book *The Vision—An Antidote to Post-*

*Charismatic Depression* I endeavour to make this point. There are things in the Bible we call biblical, because they are things that are pleasing to God. There are things we call unbiblical, because they are in the Bible but God disapproves of them. There are a lot of other things that are nonbiblical. That is, they are not directly approved of or disapproved of by God anywhere in Scripture.

Nowhere do we find Bible texts for Sunday schools, youth clubs, women's meetings, church buildings; it is questionable whether there are any texts for parachurch organisations, publishing houses and the like. But under the general umbrella of 'by all means save some' we are given freedom to employ any methods providing they do not violate principles of togetherness, church, the body of Christ and recognised leadership.

This is also true with manifestations of the Holy Spirit or indeed reactions to the Spirit's presence. As it happens there is plenty of biblical data regarding these manifestations or reactions to the Holy Spirit.

My flesh trembles in fear of you;
 I stand in awe of your laws (Psalm 119:120).

Serve the Lord with fear
 and rejoice with trembling (Psalm 2:11).

I came to you in weakness and fear,
 and with much trembling (1 Corinthians 2:3).

'Should you not fear me?' declares the Lord.
'Should you not tremble in my presence?' (Jeremiah 5:22).

While Ezra was praying and confessing, weeping
and throwing himself down before the house of
God, a large crowd of Israelites—men, women

and children—gathered round him. They too
wept bitterly (Ezra 10:1).

They will come with weeping;
 they will pray as I bring them back.
I will lead them beside streams of water
 on a level path where they will not stumble
 (Jeremiah 31:9).

'Even now,' declares the Lord,
 'return to me with all your heart,
 with fasting and weeping and mourning.' (Joel 2:12)

These men are not drunk, as you suppose. It's only
 nine in the morning! (Acts 2:15)

Eli thought Hannah was drunk and Saul certainly
appeared unusual when he stripped off his robes
and lay that way all day and night (1 Samuel 19:24).

The One enthroned in heaven laughs (Psalm 2:4).

The Lord laughs at the wicked,
 for he knows their day is coming (Psalm 37:13).

The righteous will see and fear;
 they will laugh at him (Psalm 52:6).

Blessed are you who weep now, for you will laugh
 (Luke 6:21).

When the Lord bought back the captives to Zion,
 we were like men who dreamed.

Our mouths were filled with laughter,
our tongues with songs of joy (Psalm 126:1–2).

But all of that and a lot of other biblical material besides will not satisfy the biblically religious. They suggest that some of the things happening in churches today are not exactly the same as the incidents these biblical verses refer to. But this nit-picking approach is so unscriptural. They are not so concerned about laughter in the home, or in personal discussions. It is laughter in the church!

I was invited to a summit meeting on the 'Toronto Blessing', with 26 senior evangelical leaders. Biblical objectivity went out of the window. Dismissive, sceptical and cynical asides were made, even down to assessing and judging the motives of people who queued up for blessing or went to Toronto. As I understand it, we are allowed to judge one another's behaviour, but we are not allowed to judge one another's motives. I have a difficult enough time judging my own motives and what I do—we should have little time for judging other people's motives! It is a dangerous thing to do.

But Pharisees lacking in grace are very good at judging everyone else's behaviour. They assessed that Jesus' ministry was motivated not in heaven, but from hell itself.

It is interesting to note that when John, probably Jesus' best friend, spoke of His glory, he gave us the constituent elements. He explained that Christ was 'full of grace and truth' (John 1:14). The order is of interest. Grace first, truth second. Truth without grace is a killer, just as grace without truth will eventually lead to decay and death. But our Lord on one occasion explained that He was the sum total of all reality. That grace attracted people to Him so that He could speak the truth in love.

## Truth and lies

There is a well-known publication in which I and many of my friends have often been written up quite inaccurately. The writers and publishers claim to be prophetic. I have written to them on several occasions about inaccurate, third-rate journalism. I have rarely received a reply. I have asked to see them, but those appointments have never taken place. Prophets often feel they are guardians of the nation's morals and theology.

It was Winston Churchill who commented that truth is such a valuable commodity it sometimes has to be surrounded by lies to be protected. This may be a view in the realm of politics, espionage and the military. But it is not one of the core values of Scripture!

The aforementioned magazine writers have very many concerns for the church, and wish to apply scriptural truth to those areas. But they seem unwilling for scriptural truth to be applied to inaccurate writings as they report on events at which they were not even present.

It is amazing but perhaps not surprising, how people are willing to apply the law and Scripture to everybody else, but seem not to apply it to themselves. According to Jesus that is Pharisaism.

## Conclusion

Religion and rules were necessary before Christ and the Holy Spirit. But now the Messiah has come, He wants to give us a new heart, renew our minds and put us into a network of relationships Paul refers to as the body of Christ.

True freedom, to remain free, must carry with it a

sense of responsibility for God and others around us. Otherwise it will turn to irresponsible licence and do damage to the name of our Saviour and to those in the church of Christ and beyond.

We must distinguish between temporary works and the building. Jesus said that if we seek after His kingdom, that is His rule, He would build His church. He gives us equipment to help us build but we must not confuse the equipment with the building itself. Hold on to temporary works loosely.

There is a major difference between behaviour regulated by law and behaviour regulated by grace. It may appear to be the same, but its motivation and source are completely different.

Watch out for the Pharisees who want to apply the law and Scripture but who are distanced from many parts of Scripture regarding love, life, relationships and generosity. It was Mark Twain who said, 'It is not the parts of the Bible I do not understand that bother me; it is the parts of the Bible I do understand that bother me!'

Jesus is our hero when it comes to nonreligious Christianity. He honoured Scripture and fulfilled the law. Yet He continually, and it appears somewhat deliberately, cut across Jewish traditions both in the synagogue, on the Sabbath and it seems in as many areas as He could think of! Shocking situations need to be addressed by shocking people in sometimes shocking language.

Does that mean that nonreligious people are completely lawless then? Is this teaching simply a reflection of the spirit of the age?

# CHAPTER 5

# HOW TO STAY NONRELIGIOUS

There are only two specific references to religion in the whole of the New Testament.

The first is where Paul is defending himself before King Agrippa. Speaking of his life prior to his conversion to Christ he explained that he was brought up a strict Pharisee, which was the most demanding branch of Jewish religion (Acts 26:5). He makes no reference to the moral quality or usefulness of the religion, simply that he was totally committed to it.

The second appears in a short letter James wrote to the twelve scattered tribes of Judaism.

Anyone who sets himself up as 'religious' by talking a good game is self-deceived. This kind of religion is hot air and only hot air. Real religion, the kind that passes muster before God the Father is this: reach out to the homeless and loveless in their plight, guard against corruption from the Godless world.[1]

James is clearly bursting the bubble that religious behaviour can create. This is very much tongue in cheek. He is clearly saying if you want to engage in a religion that pleases God in heaven, help the homeless, the poor,

---

1 James 1:26–27 in *The Message*.

the disenfranchised and the powerless. This is good religion! It is interesting to note that this has nothing to do with special buildings, vestments, liturgical practices, creeping around in services and even singing charismatic songs, clapping, waving one's hands in the air and having a more informal approach to worship.

His second point conveys something rather important. He tells the Jewish church to guard against the corrupting influence of the world. He moves on in the next chapter to explain that we shouldn't treat people differently because they are dressed smartly or apparently have a lot of money. People are different and need to be treated differently. But that doesn't mean they are special in a hierarchical sense, so that it is wrong to treat those with social graces and wealth in a special way, and believers who live in council houses, or who may also be unemployed and virtually penniless, with disregard.

One of my main problems with the so-called 'faith' teaching is an impression that the Spirit-filled life should lead from one mountain-top experience to another, on some sort of invisible bridge. Now it is true that writers explain that Jesus was on occasions full of joy. He hadn't simply got joy, He was full of joy. You can almost see His teeth as He throws His head back and roars with laughter. But He was also a man of sorrows and acquainted with grief, betrayed, lied to and robbed. There were times when His own disciples didn't understand who He was or what He had come to do. So he lived a Spirit-filled life, between the tension of joy and grief, gain and loss, laughter and tears.

Not all 'faith' ministries are the same. They have been much maligned. Some have shifted their emphasis of teaching. We should be careful not to write off preachers and teachers because of an odd line we have heard about their teaching or because of matters of style.

But it is interesting that most faith teachers are white, male, middle-aged or late middle-aged, middle class or higher middle class. Most are not personally involved in Rwanda, former Yugoslavia or with the church in China, India, or parts of South America, all going through untold suffering. Heading up large organisations and operating in television, training and education and large meetings, such teachers can easily become detached from the world that most Christians face at work or college and university. The only time many preachers and particularly those in the 'faith' ministry face unconverted people is at the end of the meeting when they want to give their lives to Christ.

## Faith, failure and suffering

But the unhealthy, albeit unintentional, emphasis of much faith preaching is the notion that the spiritual life takes you up and out of reality, and brings you to a place of regular heady ecstasies. Prayer is easy, angels are nearby, miracles are there for the taking, little can go wrong. It is not the picture that Jesus or His follower the Apostle Paul paints. Reading through the narratives there were relational bust-ups, personal failures, prison, torture, interrogation, hunger and thirst, physical beatings and betrayals. Both Jesus and Paul allude to the fact they got tired and depressed, discouraged and frustrated. We see it particularly with Jesus in the garden of Gethsemane. We see it in Paul's travels and with members of his team.

We are to guard against the corruption of the world around us that causes us to see people other than how our Lord sees them. We are to guard against putting a value on people, related to fame, position, money and social graces.

But Paul does not say that we are to withdraw from the world, live life in Christian meetings, only meet with Christian people and do Christian, religious things. Quite the opposite is true when we read of Paul's passion for the lost.

And that's it: two mentions of religion—one referring to Judaism and another to practical care for the poor and powerless.

## This is not new

One of the earliest mentions of the phrase 'religionless Christianity' this century is by Bonhoeffer in a letter to his friend Eberhard Bethge. It was probably written in the late thirties. He endeavoured to bring out the difference between faith and religion. You can be religious without having any faith in God. More importantly, you can have faith in God without being religious.

Religion involves a part of our lives on specific occasions on special days. Faith engages the whole person all the time. The call of Christ is not to a new religion but a new life.

It is my contention that nonreligious Christians are by implication neither religious nor irreligious. Religion is normally a cover for something else and that something else is normally dark, unclean and will nearly always be found on the wrong side of God. It need not be so but as Jesus Christ indicated, it normally is!

Neither have we got to be irreligious. Any half-inebriated debauchee can cry 'freedom' while being addicted to drink and tobacco, to flirtation and lust. The main issue with the freedom Christ gives us has to relate to what we are doing to do with that freedom. Are we going to end up like any irreligious, blasphemous, addicted cynic? Or are we going to do something else with our freedom?

That freedom allows us to be with religious people without harshly judging them all the time. We are free to be with them, and hopefully draw them out into something more liberating, healthy and whole. Equally, our freedom allows us to model a different quality of life to the irreligious with its attendant irresponsibility and lack of care for others. We are free! We are even free to relate to the religious and the irreligious without becoming either ourselves.

## Religion and heaven

Somebody once remarked to another, 'Won't it be good when we are all in heaven. The Roman Catholics will be able to eat meat on a Friday!' The listener responded, 'Yes, it will also be a place where the Jews can eat pork chops all day long!' There was lots of laughter. The initiator of the conversation picked it up again: 'Heaven will also be a place where evangelicals can drink in front of each other!' (more laughter!) There are all sorts of things that religion hinders people from doing openly. Secret drinking generally means there are other secret areas of our lives. It is the secret areas of our lives where Jesus is not Lord.

So how can we remain nonreligious without being unnecessarily corrupted by the world around us?

## Become a lover of the truth

Truth does not need personality to make it beautiful or numbers to reinforce it. Truth has a beauty and power of its own.

We live in an age where truth is devalued. Even in our places of supposed education, there are those who teach that there is no such thing as truth and, by implication, morality.

*Time* magazine carried a feature article suggesting that we had done ourselves no favours by allowing schools to take over the traditional family task of teaching ethics, morals and values.[2] How can such things be taught without reference to God?

Ethics are based on an ancient belief that there are supernatural forces at work which provide a framework for ethics and moral responsibility.

But many school teachers and college/university professors tell us that we cannot go back to a world where ethics can be based on a revelation of what God requires of us. One explains, 'Nor can we reasonably expect people to behave morally by exercising free will. Free will simply doesn't exist. Genetic and environmental factors do not merely influence our moral decisions, they determine them.'[3]

But this philosophy is blind to reality and it is also self-defeating. He pulls the rug from under his feet when he says that we are not free. If he genuinely believes that he would not be trying to convince his students to change the way they think. That implies that they are free to change!

If they are not free to respond to their own thoughts why should they be free to respond to his? If this is a sample of modern education, we are in serious trouble. It implies that we are not responsible for our behaviour, but our genetic code is.

Seven years after this was written, *Time* magazine published one of the most fascinating but dangerous

---

2   *Time* magazine, 26 May 1987.
3   *Time* magazine, 26 May 1987, page 61.

articles I have ever read. I take *Time* on a weekly basis; I regard it to be the best weekly news magazine in the world. But on 15 August 1994 ten pages were devoted to biogenetic ethics under the title 'Infidelity: It May Be in Our Genes'.

There were no footnotes giving any foundation to these ideas. There was barely a single reference as to how biological factors influenced our sexual impulses. This is how the writer explains the romance and love:

The good news is that human beings are designed to fall in love. The bad news is that they aren't designed to stay there . . . it is natural . . . to commit adultery . . . It is similarly natural to find some attractive colleague superior on all counts to the sorry wreck of a spouse you are saddled with.[4]

Perhaps the author Richard Wright failed to document scientific conclusions, simply because they do not exist. Colleagues in the field of biogenetic research have responded by saying that for the foreseeable future the results of certain findings will continue to hinge on assumptions of questionable validity. Many acknowledge that human sexuality is a very complex subject and cannot be reduced to genetic causes alone.

Of course if we teach our children that we are merely animals, albeit morally superior to the snake and the cow, we shouldn't be surprised if they act like animals.

Truth is vitally important. We must become lovers of truth, not simply with respect to abstract ideas, but truth rooted in our own morality, human relationships and our approach to work and areas of responsibility. Truth does not need a bulldozer to make its point nor a poison-

---

4   *Time* magazine, 15 August 1994, page 46.

tipped arrow to make its mark. Truth has its own way of becoming seed that bears fruit. Truth can be rejected but it cannot be changed.

If we fail to be lovers of truth, we will be lovers of our own agendas, perspectives, prejudices, scepticism and cynical nature. Either that or we shall become so detached from reality we will not be able to interact with anyone who has got their feet on the earth and their heart in heaven.

## Faith and doubt

### Practise the presence of God
The Methodist ministry E. Stanley Jones once remarked that the difference between the East and the West is that the East was wondering which God to believe in whilst the West was wondering if there was a God at all.

The church is full of silent doubters. One of the most important issues today is to deal with the doubts amongst our own young adults and the grown ups! Doubts are often created by our modern world. They can hide behind religion.

Religion doesn't interact with TV channels, sweet perfume, sexual imagery, board-room discussions and our leisure reading. At best it disengages from the lot although in reality, living in the world we do, it is an impossibility. Denial becomes the only route, along with its attendant dishonesty.

Faith on the other hand can engage and access the value of all those things. Practising the presence of Christ in life (as against in special buildings on special days) will determine what I watch on television and how much I watch. It will influence what I read and why I read it. It will influence my response to tempting smells and sounds, shapes and textures. Faith is for life.

Practise the presence of God in a conversation, either while you are speaking or listening. We may be surprised at how often God speaks to us so that when we would rather speak, we are more inclined to listen. When we are likely to duck out of an issue through cowardice we find grace and courage to speak up.

One can be a fully paid-up tongues-speaking charismatic, meeting in a hired facility with a five-piece band and no hint of anything which is outwardly religious. But if what happens on a Sunday morning when we break bread (or at any other time!) doesn't affect how we treat one another for the rest of the day, we are into religion, not faith. If we can walk away from a meeting which is filled with the presence of God and manifestations of the Holy Spirit and gossip over lunch or watch a blood-letting violent film, blasphemous comedian or sexually explicit feature film without a tinge of conscience, we are into religion. If we can sing of God's grace with furrowed brow and mega sincere heart and mercilessly judge those who are different from us or who have hurt us, we are into religion.

## Etiquette and religion

We live in an age where decency and etiquette pass for virtuous integrity. We also live in an age where deception, corruption and illusion pass for pardonable imperfections.

Conniving becomes entrepreneurial! Respectability becomes Christianity. Apologies are confused for repentance. This is the world of the flat-souled; it is inoffensive, safe and dangerous as hell.

There is a loss of urgency for the unconverted, a lack

of genuine, generous respect for leaders and what we have here is religion, ten miles wide and one inch deep.

Religion does not want to be inconvenienced. Practising the presence of Christ in the complex issues of life will inconvenience us. It is fight or flight.

It was said prior to the Second World War that Britain continued to 'take its weekends in the country while Hitler takes his countries in the weekends'. Suggestions that weekends be shortened, or that provision should be made for emergency, was met with silence or shocked disbelief.

The idea that God is in a hurry and we should be in a hurry is lacking in respectability also.

Even among Christians, this lack of practising the presence of God reduces some of the most serious issues of life down to mere problems. We have a school sex problem; the not unrelated AIDS problem; a rape problem; a drink problem; a drug problem; the selfish society problem; the militant Muslim problem. There are few people who are willing to come forward and explain in open terms that some if not all of these things are wrong.

To the Christian many of these problems are not within our small network of loving, kind, snug friends. So we do not grieve over stories of civil war and torture, starvation and famine. We continue with our superficial cheeriness and we conform to a set of ideals and feelings which can be found in the house next door, full of agnostics or unbelievers.

Cornelius Plantinga Junior has pointed out that this approach to life's issues is a narcotic, a tranquillising and disorientating suppression of our spiritual central nervous system. He writes:

What is devastating about it is that when we lack an

ear for wrong notes in our lives, we cannot play right ones or even recognise them in the performance of others. Eventually we make ourselves religiously so tone deaf that we miss both the exposition and recapitulation of the main themes God plays in human life.

The music of creation and the still greater music of grace whistle right through our skulls, causing no catch of the breath and leaving no residue. Moral beauty begins to bore us. The idea that the human race needs a saviour sounds quaint.[5]

Failure to practise the presence of Christ in the whole of life and particularly in our relationships together, will leave us rejecting in principle what we actually do in practice.

## Religion-free mission

### Ask God to give you a heart for the lost

Over 100 years ago Dr A. B. Simpson coined the phrase 'bring back the King'. It inspired thousands to a passionate commitment to complete the great commission and launch a world-wide movement so that the nations were networked with the gospel.

Jesus Christ led us to believe that the gospel must reach all people groups before He returned.

Staying with it, that is what God requires. Stay with it to the end. You won't be sorry and you will be saved. All during this time the good news, the

---

5 Cornelius Plantinga Junior, *Not the Way it is Supposed to Be: A Breviary of Sin* (Eardmans).

message of the Kingdom will be preached all over the world, a witness staked out in every country and then the end will come.[6]

According to the US Centre for World Mission, in the year AD 1430 only one in one hundred people were Bible-believing Christians. By 1790 it was one in forty-nine; by 1940 one in thirty-two; by 1980 one in sixteen and by 1995 one in nine.[7]

I confess, many years ago I tired of reading charts and books about the second coming, which emphasised calamity, the Jews, rebuilding of the temple and all the other end-time themes most of us are so familiar with. The main eschatological emphasis of Jesus' ministry is summed up in Matthew chapter 24 which we have just read. It is astonishing that the religious, often caught up with such escapist themes, have never invited a neighbour or colleague home for a meal, and have rarely shared their faith in an attractive and intelligible form. I say this after 25 years of observing my own and other people's behaviour when it comes to the gospel.

We are not all evangelists. I am not primarily an evangelist. I have younger men and women around me who can communicate the gospel more succinctly, clearly and persuasively then I have ever done. But in the last few years I have been deeply challenged about my own lack of contact with the unconverted, those who are not yet Christians. I even had to change my phraseology, as I was prone to refer to all those neighbours and acquaintances who had not yet committed their life to Christ as 'non-Christians'. I have even been at evangelistic meetings where the convener has welcomed 'non-Christians'.

---

6  Matthew 24:14, in *The Message*.
7  Figures supplied by Lausanne Statistical Task Force headed by Dave Barratt Ph.D.

It is the nearest thing to saying that is a 'non-person'. I started to use the phrase 'not-yet-Christian'. Of course that can end up as lazy shorthand, sloganeering jargon if you like. But I believe it is much nearer the heart of God to say that a person is not yet a Christian, which implies movement and possibility, than non-Christian which is static and almost final.

It has been said that there is nothing like a dose of experience to change one's theology. Whilst not subscribing to that view, there is sufficient truth in it for it to be troublesome. My own life was increasingly taken up with my Christian wife and my three sons, all of whom have faith. I work with a group of leaders in my church Pioneer People. Some are on the oversight, caring for the whole church, twenty-six are on a Senior Leadership Team and a larger number in the Leaders' Forum. Each are born-again, Spirit-filled Christians with whom I have a great deal of respect. Outside those local relationships and responsibilities I have a national Pioneer Team, who care for churches, plant churches and train leaders and evangelists. So I am involved in a wide range of team days, training programmes and speaking in the churches and at leadership groups within our network of Pioneer-related churches. Some of my time is spent behind my desk, writing books, scripts for films, and responding to a never-ending flow of mail, invitations and reading matter. By about two years ago, I had arrived at such dizzy heights of Christian fame and function that my contact with those who are not yet Christian was limited to a few words with the milkman, the gas metre reader and the occasional shouting match through the glass partition with a taxi driver. That was it.

The only answer for me was to change my lifestyle. I love Christian fellowship, so whenever I could I invited Christian friends around to our home for a meal, for fellowship or a video. My life was filled with Christian people and events.

With my conscience pricked and prodded, whenever we naturally reached for our phone to invite Christian friends around, we stopped. 'How about the next-door neighbours or a relative?' we asked. Slowly we invited neighbours, relatives and acquaintances to our home. They, in return, invited us back to their homes, and there we met new friends as yet who had never ever heard the gospel and probably had not seen 'normal' Christians.

After two years of turning down meetings in order to spend time with neighbours, and repenting of Christian clubbiness (with some very good, faithful Christian friends) I almost feel as though I have rejoined the human race.

In such settings one cannot talk about the church, theology, the meeting last Sunday, the event last month, the Toronto Blessing or our favourite Christian superstars and heroes. It was quite a challenge. I have had to make room in my heart and diary for those whom Jesus came to save and redeem to Himself. I will not pretend, this has not been easy. It has been a sacrifice and we see less of many of our close friends in order to break the recurring cycle of safe, predictable fellowship.

If we are to have viable churches amongst all people groups we have to face the fact that even in our own nation there are unreached people. It could be the road you live in or it could be a relational group such as youth. The list is endless.

If we are to read the Bible for all its worth, Scripture teaches us that faith is for others as well as for ourselves.

The need around us is sometimes so great it can paralyse us into retreat, into religion and into a cosy, self-satisfied mind-set that we think will immunise us from the pain of reality.

## Cold statistics and warm people

What are we going to do with the people represented by the following statistics?

- 80% of the 185,000 divorces a year are initiated by wives. 66% of these cite 'unreasonable behaviour'. Custody or 'residence' of children is nearly always granted to the wife; conduct of the parties is generally deemed irrelevant. A husband who may be innocent of all alleged misconduct is obliged to support his ex-wife and their children and may well be served with an order to leave the home and his children. Britain has the highest divorce rate in Europe. Over half a million men, women and children have already been directly affected by divorce in the last twelve months.

- The Family Health Services authority of the Cornwall and Isles of Scilly district recently approved a budget for the county's GPs to provide free condoms and contraceptive advice for children aged between 13 and 18. Parents will not be informed. The annual cost will be almost £15,000. The fee for GPs will be almost £20,000.

- The New Harvard School of Public Health study reckons that HIV threatens to infect as many as 120 million people by the end of the century. This doubles previous predictions.

I would suggest that most addictions to alcohol, gambling, forays into crime and sexual activity could be traced back to the family or lack of it. The statistics in themselves are awful, but there is much more lying behind the statistics that is not picked up in the figures I have quoted. Some families appear to be together when they are not; they are being ripped apart by addictions and illusions. They do not live somewhere else, they live in your road, and they are a part of the network of relationships or acquaintances we meet in front of the local school, in the supermarket or at work.

In the church I lead we have asked God to help us see people the way He sees them. At times I wish I hadn't prayed that prayer, nor that we have continued to pray it. I can only describe what has happened as an inward groan that at times cannot even be uttered. I wake up with it, I sometimes lie awake in bed at night with it. It can be crowded out by fun and friendship, a busy diary or holidays. But as we go on praying that prayer, God has His own way of helping us to see people as lost, severe wrongdoers who have resisted grace and truth. It breaks your heart.

The pain of a lost world causes us to question a lot of our activity. This need not be from a cynical viewpoint but in terms of how fruitful we have been in sowing the seed of the gospel, watering it with our prayers and seeing a harvest. It brings us back to reality.

Simone Weil made a brilliant observation:

Nothing is so beautiful, nothing is so continually fresh and surprising, so full of sweet and perpetual ecstasy as the good; no desert is so dreary, monotonous and boring as evil. But with fantasy it is the other way around. Fictional good is boring and flat, while fictional evil is varied, intriguing, attractive and full of charm.

These words were written several years before television had been developed to attract its colossal audiences across the world. Celebrity status, fame and success are the goals of life rather than a broken and contrite heart.
Malcolm Muggeridge added:

The transposition of good and evil in the world of fantasy created by the media leaves us with no sense of moral order in the universe and without this, no order whatsoever, social, political, economic or any other, is ultimately attainable.[8]

Television has changed how and why we elect our leaders. Image is far more important than reality. We live in a world dominated by the media; it draws us into a process where desensitisation slowly takes place. The viewer or listener needs more and more or we shall get stimulated less and less.

We are, in the words of another, 'amusing ourselves to death'. Ravi Zacharias the apologist has commented that the whole concept of sitting in a dark room, staring at an illuminated box and demanding that everyone in the room is silent, ought to make for a serious psychological enquiry!

But it is amazing that people can literally loathe television programmes, castigate their own viewing habits, agree that hours and hours of television is probably not doing their children any good and then think it is

---

8  Malcolm Muggeridge, *Christ and the Media*, page 46.

completely bazarre should anyone suggest that they get rid of the TV. Perhaps we shouldn't be surprised that Vladimir Kosma Zworykin, the Russian-born inventor of television, commented on his 92nd birthday, 'I would never let my children even come close to this thing,' referring to his invention.

We should not be surprised therefore with children, teenagers and young adults weaned on hours and hours of television (at a most conservative estimate 30–40 hours a week, a mere 5 hours a day/evening) that they find reality difficult to grasp. Neither should we be surprised at the end results of allowing, and positively promoting, the medium of myth and fantasy to desensitise from reality.

The situation reminds me of the man who commented 'I just got my dog to a place where it could survive without food and it died!'

Perhaps no civilisation in history has so flagrantly, happily and deliberately flaunted its mediocre culture, moral shallowness and unclean spirit.

The answer to all of this is not religion, as an escape for the faithful minority, but faith in Christ. He gives us life and relationships. The age to come is not full of religion, but life. Heaven is not a place full of religious rectitude, but unbridled happiness.

Following Christ does not mean dragging our past around with us, not even our religious past. It is grabbing a hold of the future, a nonreligious, bright, open future and dragging it into the here and now.

Thank you Jesus for modelling nonreligious Christianity. What freedom!

# CHAPTER 6

# CONCLUSION

Religion is only spoken of in terms of helping the 'homeless and loveless' in the New Testament. It never speaks of religion as going to church, singing or prayer all typified by special robes, altars and calendars. Indeed, New Testament 'religion' is practical, caring and self-sacrificing. By today's definition and understanding of the word, it is barely a religion at all. Religion, as currently understood, encourages escape, unreality and is often a cover for the group dynamics of manipulation and control. However, faith encourages us to face life head on; it embraces reality, with all of its pain.

We live in a world of myths, fantasy and illusion. Television, watched by the vast majority for many hours a week, is a considerable influence in reinforcing value systems. It could be argued that tabloid newspapers, read by the majority of people, are even worse. Both have made goodness, faithfulness, integrity and purity flat and boring. They have made violence, unfaithfulness, fame, riches and even evil exciting, inviting and in many cases addictive. It caused one British journalist, reviewing the newspapers on breakfast television, to comment, 'How would we fill the newspapers if we all behaved ourselves?' Much of television and the tabloids turn Christian values on their head.

Religion is helpless when faced with this topsy-turvy world. It often serves simply as an escape. Religion also encourages spiritual smugness. That is a condition which leaves us satisfied with skimpy results, often of exaggerated importance.

Christians are therefore likely to have their values derived either from the media (particularly television and the tabloids) or so-called Christian religion with its attendant inoffensive niceness. With the former we live in two worlds, with two value systems, and are likely to become spiritually schizophrenic. With the latter, we cannot face a robust pagan world. On one occasion Jesus stood up and proclaimed He was the truth. In the original language that can be translated as 'I am the sum total of all reality.' The concept of God, His Christ and the work of the Holy Spirit is the most important topic of theology and practical Christian living. It is therefore from Scripture that we must derive our understanding of what the Christian faith is about.

We need to nurture churches where people are allowed to be real and where people are allowed to sin. That does not mean encouraged to sin, or that there should be churches that condone sin. But if we build churches which do not allow people to sin, they have to cover up. Instead of the church becoming a focus of reality, openness and vulnerability, it becomes the arena for its own myths, fantasies and cover-ups.

Don't be fooled by me, by the face I wear
For I wear a mask
Pretending is an art that is second nature to me, but
  don't be fooled
I give the impression that I am secure, that all is
  merry and unruffled with me
That confidence is my name and coolness is my
  game
My surface may seem very smooth, but my surface
  is my mask

Beneath lies the real me,
In confusion, in fear and aloneness
But I hide this
I don't want anyone to know
I create a mask to hide behind
A nonchalant, sophisticated facade
To help me pretend, to shield from a glance that
  knows
But such a glance is my salvation
If it is followed by love, it is the only thing that can
  liberate me from myself
From my own self-built prison walls
From the barriers I so painstakingly erect
It is the only thing that can assure me of what I can't
  assure myself
That I am really worth something
But I don't tell you this—I wouldn't dare to
I'm afraid to
I'm afraid you'll think less of me
And that you will reject me
So I play my game—my desperate pretending game
I idly chatter to you in suave surface talk
And I tell you everything of what is nothing
And nothing of what is everything
Of what is crying within me
So when I go through my routine don't be fooled by
  what I'm saying
I dislike the superficial game I'm playing
I'd like to be genuine and spontaneous
But you've got to help me, to hold out your hand
Only you can wipe away from my eyes the blank
  stare of the breathing dead
Only you can call me into aliveness each time you
  are kind and gentle and encouraging
Each time you try to understand

With sensitivity and sympathy and your power of
  understanding you can breathe life into me
Do not pass me by
It won't be easy, a long conviction of worthlessness
  and strong walls
I fight against the very thing I cry out for
But I am told that love is stronger than walls
And in this lies my only hope
Who am I?—you may wonder
I am every man you met
And I am every woman you meet.

Author unknown

# Out of the Ghetto and Into the City

## Patrick Dixon

This book is a radical call to get involved in the community, from a doctor involved in both social action and church planting.

'More people found faith last year, worldwide, than in any other year in the history of the world—but as churches grow, will nations be transformed? Recent "times of refreshing" are for service. Jesus is calling us to leave the comfort of our Christian ghettos, and follow Him into the city, as salt and light, making a difference wherever we go. Social action is a prophetic demonstration of the love of God.'

Catalogue Number YB 9737

£3.99

# Christian Citizenship

## Mike Morris

What is Christian Citizenship? It is more than the privilege of individual salvation, we are told in this Pioneer *Perspective*. It is also about the responsibility to serve the local community and being loving to our neighbours.

We are challenged on our own particular lifestyle. Do we reflect our relationship with Christ in every sphere? As Jesus did, we must stand alongside the poor and marginalised, meet their needs, refuse to conform to cultural stereotypes and be prepared to challenge authority where necessary.

After presenting the biblical context—the provision made for the poor and aliens in the Old Testament, the balancing-up process of the Jubilee and Jesus' two greatest commandments—the author outlines how Christians can be empowered to put their faith into action, by establishing relationships within the community and ensuring that the roles of prophet, politician and pastor are all filled.

Catalogue Number YB 9734                    £3.99